MYSTICS OF LOVE

LOVE IS THE FIRST STEP TOWARDS THE DIVINE

'KAILASHI' PUNIT D. SHARMA &
SHEENA CHOUDHARY

ISBN 979-888555083-3

OM

RESPECTED TEACHERS & PAPA MUMMY

DEAR MAAHI, KALRAV, SANKHYA, PURVAI, VEDANT

TUSHI & ANNU

BETTER HALF LAVINA

INDU DIDI, DR. PANKAJ JIYAJI, VINIT & GARIMA

DEAR FRIENDS, COLLEAGUES & READERS

Contents

Contents

Foreword

EDITOR - SHIVANI BHATIA

Mystics Of Love by Mr. 'KAILASHI' Punit D. Sharma and Miss Sheena Choudhary offer a wonderful insight into the world of love. Love, as an emotion has been always astonishing to the human soul. We are always lured by the notion of love. This particular compilation takes us on a remarkable journey. Our heart experiences countless aches of happiness, sorrow, excitement, and anger. In fact, the book is a roller coaster ride of emotions. As the title suggests, poems weave an intricate web of mystic love. Both the authors delve passionately into the realm of love. On one hand, Mr. Sharma indulges in intense fabricating of platonic love. His poems captivate our soul as it stirs our idea of love. On the other hand, Miss Sheena constructs an engaging feminine reflection of love. Her love passes through banal reality to celestial emotions.

These love poems touch strings of the soul. They proffer us an elixir of love. Mystics Of Love is a splendid collection of lucid and pungent poems devising a new universe of love for us. Readers are definitely going to enjoy this compilation. These love words will diffuse into their blood melting their soul profusely. I wish both authors the best of luck with a brilliant compilation.

Shivani Bhatia
M.A. , M.Phil. (English)
AECC Guest Faculty
Delhi School of Journalism,
The University of Delhi, New Delhi, India.

About The Editor

Shivani Bhatia is the AECC Guest Faculty at the Delhi School of Journalism, University of Delhi. She has received her M.Phil., centered around Raja Rao's novels. She has also cleared NET and SET exams in English. Prior to taking up her current assignment, she has been a part of the academic staff at such prestigious institutions like IIT Delhi, NIT Delhi, Jamia Millia Islamia Delhi, and VJTI Mumbai. During her nine years of teaching experience, she has taught various courses and students from different strata as well. She has an immense interest in reading and writing poetry. For her, poetry is the foundation of life. It opens the gateway to all our senses and awakens our souls.

Preface

Love is the first step towards the divine...and surrender is the last and these two steps are the whole journey. The whole universe is created through one and only one ingredient i.e. true love of nature. Nature has created everything based on true, unconditional, and divine love, that's why every creation is complete in the true sense. The completeness is been felt only through the path of true love. See around and feel why and how nature creates and nurtures each and every species on this planet unconditionally. Nature's creations are complete because the cause behind them is beyond profit-loss & give-take analysis and is based on divine love and sacrifice. We humans live with nature, surrounded by it and feeling it but never imbibe, and if we imbibe it then this is the complete salvation.

The book is filled with interpretations of love in its various forms and provides a peek into how one emotion can have such stark variations in its interpretations, understanding, and experiences.

On the one end, Mr. Kailashi has brought a very mature outlook on the love of other kinds- love for God, love for nature, and love for oneself. On the other end, Ms. Sheena looks at love as a powerful force. It is for the readers to assess for themselves whether this force is constructive or destructive in nature.

Both writing styles are different yet amalgamate beautifully in this collection of poems. They transport you to multiple realms. The readers can visualize what they read.

Preface

Love [illegible] the divine, and surrender is the [illegible] beg[illegible] the [illegible] journey. The whole universe is created [illegible] radiant [illegible] of nature [illegible] [illegible] the complete[illegible] is [illegible] of true [illegible]. [illegible] and feel [illegible] and [illegible] every [illegible] [illegible] beyond [illegible] [illegible] and sacrifice. We [illegible] [illegible] the [illegible]

This book is filled with interpretations [illegible] and provides a peek into [illegible] such words, variations [illegible] interpretations [illegible] understanding [illegible] [illegible]

[illegible]

Prologue

The natural and overarching inclination of these poems strung together is love and strength through her poems, Sheena offers a feminine gaze into their idea of love. She rustles through paper and paper cuts, while constantly reaching out to the mundane things for inspiration. She believes that every poem of hers is a work in progress and never complete. The poems are a collection of twigs and thoughts from 2015 onwards. Almost too self-conscious to come out of their shells, these poems have been comforting her sadness- as a means of catharsis and companionship. Most poems in this section - You smirking evil, Bad O' Bad, When the red flowers bloom, Colour of love, When two people meet, Farewell, The missed call, I have forgotten my lover, and Arrival talk about jittery love, messy heartbreaks and the unsaid expectations that go through a lover's mind. They tread around the memories of their beloved gently. The writing displays sadness and constant successful and unsuccessful attempts of the heart in processing the love, guilt, hurt, and grief like tug and war.

Others like Deviants and Canadian Summer have resulted in themselves out of exasperation by the social systems and expectations. Some like paradox, as the name suggests, tie up womanhood with the roles women play, their multitudes, and how they bounce back in the face of adversity.

Poems written by Mr. Kailashi Puneet Sharma are the English translations of his original Hindi work that encompasses themes of love, life, and the spiritual side of the same. His poems hit a different note. You can find his original Hindi poems in a collection called Kavyanjali. His poems force you to reflect deep and hard about life as we know it, shattering the notions of our own grandeur, while also grounding the reader with the beauty of thoughts and words alike. His poems about love paint the picture of spring where nature comes alive to embrace the earth. They seem like written for the love- of people and God- making his poems a spiritual experience to read.

Both the authors in this book provide the readers with two sides of love. One is shattered, romantic, and hopeful like early stages of love are. Others have evolved out of their romantic form and are spiritual and secure in how it sees their lover- that is the God, godly things, and people themselves.

About The Authors

'KAILASHI' Punit D. Sharma

Kailashi Punit D. Sharma is associated with administrative statistics and planning by profession, he started writing after the Kailash Mansarovar Yatra in 2015. His first poetic work, 'Kavyanjali- Jeevan Ek moun abhivayakti' (life is a silent expression), has been published, in this book, he summarized the various aspects of the journey of life. The compositions are presented, some of these compositions which show divinity with the love of nature, have been compiled in this book.

Punit Sharma presents his poems in a satirical style and you will find a mixture of spirituality and philosophy in his poems. He is a nature lover and is the author of the bestseller book Essence Of Life 'Divide by Zero' A Scientific Approach to Sustainable Development.

In this book, readers will get to read poems highlighting various aspects of love.

It has been the effort of the authors to introduce different definitions of love to different sections of the readers and to make them see the love prevailing in the whole of nature.

UGC-NET M.A. Economics

Chief planning officer, Udaipur

Joint Director Economics & Statistics Rajasthan, India

20 Years of Work Experience- Teaching & Administrative Statistics

Sheena Choudhary

Sheena is a social worker by profession. This book is her maiden effort to bring some of her thoughts and pieces that she has jotted over the years. She aspires to work in the field of human rights broadly. She finds comfort in regular life and old Hindi songs. On a regular day, you can find her appreciating good lyrics, music, art, food, and smell. She makes good analogies and even better puns and likes to humblebrag about it. She hates small talk but is surprisingly good at it as part of adulting.

M.A. Social Work, Delhi University

UGC-NET M.A. Social Work

MGN Fellow- MSDE and IIM Banglore

4 Years of Work Experience- Social Work

1. GOOD MORNING 22

Wake Up Dear Wake Up
A nice whole day and the new year is waiting for you
A beautiful Sunshine has knocked on the door to hug you
A colorful ray has traveled thousands of miles to meet you
Look
Birds have taken bath and fly away from the nest to enjoy the beauty of nature
They are chirping and flying here and there to wake you up, aren't they provoking you to play with them?
See
Sunshine has warmed up the drops of the water in the pond, aren't tempting you to clean up your soul?
Watch
Flowers and Leaves on the plants have decorated themselves with the dew, aren't they attracting you to collect the nectar
Observe
Each and every creation of Nature is here to alive you
And you are still sleeping
And you are still celebrating the old day of the old year
Wake up dear wake up
It's the new day of the new year 2022
Let's start celebrating, the new day of the new year

with this resolution

Happy New Year 2022

2. May be You Understand

What
if you can understand
For me
look at me
within me
only for a moment
what I can't tell you
can you understand
That
some things are like this
I know I know
I know I don't know
I don't know I know
And
I don't know I don't know
That's why I Can't Explain
May Be You Better Understand
What was explained, was known
What was Understood, wasn't known
to me

3. Season of The Nature

Dear it's the weather of the sky
Let these eyes tuck
cloud-covered sky
But
missing somewhere is
Maneka's charm in the earth
Who captivates the belief of the
black clouds of the sky,
force it
to embrace Vasundhara
But
missing somewhere is
the dedication of Shivaliks in the mountains
Who has broken the modesty of the holy Bhagirathi,
force it
to embrace Vasundhara
But
missing somewhere is
Aditya's swift extradition in the fire
One who is pleased with the austerity of Aditi
to force Sushumna
to embrace Vasundhara

But
missing somewhere is
there in the sea
the dedication like Marutinandan
to force clouds
to embrace Vasudha (Mother Earth)
Dear this is the season of the Sky
Dear this is the season of the Vasudha (Mother Earth)
Darling, it's the season of the nature

4. I am I

I am I
you are you
I will explain
Until you understand
If you don't
I will continue
I gave, I give, I will give
You received, you receive, you will receive
I am the river flows, used to flow, and will continue to flow
Until your thirst completely be quenched
I am the air flows, used to flow, and will continue to flow
Until you completely are refreshed
I am the light blown, used to lighten, and will continue to lighten
Until you completely are enlightened
I am the soil nurture, used to nurture, and will continue to nurture
Until you completely are nurtured
I am the space spacious, used to be spacious, will continue to be spacious
Until you completely are specified
I am the river, the air, the light, the soil, and the space

but you are you

you are you

I am I

5. By Yourself, Why Not Love?

I didn't ask you anything
Nor did you give me anything
Whatever was offered
Accepted
Love for Love
And
Hate for Hate
Everything
I kept giving myself
And keep getting
Love for Love
And
Hate for Hate
Then why offer hate?
why not love?
I had to get
I had to give
Then why the hate?
why not love?

6. Illusion-Brahma-Param Brahma

What am I doing?
Why am I doing it?
What is happening?
Why is it happening?
Was this to do?
What is happening?
I am doing
Or is happening
It is done
Then I'm here
That I have come
Is happening again
Yesterday I was not
What was happening
Tomorrow I won't be
Will, it just be
I am nothing
You are nothing
We are nothing
Illusion, Illusion & Illusion

As soon as I am free
I am Brahma
As soon as you are free
You are Brahma
As soon as we are free
We are Brahma
Param Brahma

7. Complete Salvation

It's been a long time now
will change now
how long can we survive
how long can we bear
If the conditions were favorable, they would also be unfavorable
If it was unfavorable, it would be favorable too
but something must happen
whenever it changes
Until how long
sunshine will keep smiling
the flowers will keep on smelling
the birds will keep chirping
now something will change
Until how long
the roads will keep rolling
circumstances will keep screaming
dreams will be shattered
now something will change
when will this change last
And we're out of this change-love
will be tied
No

I don't want to change now
freedom from bondage not from life
Freedom from this change of attachment-love
I want salvation
Complete Salvation

8. Flowing Moments

To every moment
by the moment
steal it from it
or fill with
this exasperation that
someone will steal
life is flowing
moment by moment
make every single moment
your own moment
fill moment with
complete mobility
and with vigor
life is flow
of moments
one by one
passing by
one by one
endless moments
endless life
life is
flow, fly, free

9. It Is Not Two It Is One

It is not

Receiving

It is

Keep giving

It is not

final

It is

pinnacle

It is not

end

It is

bend

It is not

perfect

It is

effect

It is not

fact

It is

affact

It is not

getting

It is

loosing

It is not

suffering

It is

surfing

It is not

lonely

It is

Only

It is not

beware

It is

aware

It is not

two

It is

one

It is

one and

only one

Love

True Love

&

Unconditional Love

10. Farewell

Farewell thee well away for best
Brow/eye, no, cry no more
Lay lay those dreams to rest
Thou shall fly no more
Sulking sobbing shattered heart
Hum thy gentle lore
Throw away my love, grimmest
Over Mariana's shore

11. I Have Forgotten My Lover

I have forgotten my lover
Except for the forlorn nights
When the shivers creep in
For company under the satin (sheets)
Gone is the warmth of body and breath
And from somewhere under my ear
Emerges the sound of
Unbecoming stress knots
Letting it/the release
With a sigh.
I have forgotten my lover
But on the rainy days
When the sun is not down
Yet the evening gets chilly
I try hard to feel her presence
While I brew tea leaves to perfection
Equal parts of milk, love, and water
I miss her complaining about piling bills
Between the sounds of
Rain and thunder.

I have forgotten my lover
Yet she lingers (around)
Like a faint scent on my fingers
Of Champa and Harshingar
That I picked from the earth
Planted on her palms
In the hopes of a revival
I stretch the moments
To let her linger a bit more
A habit was gone bad.
I have forgotten my lover
But she keeps running into me
At each nook of this city
Full of bags and baggage
Of passing mentions and
Mostly good memories
Which often pass by
Loneliness is not easy either
But she is cyanide.
I have forgotten my lover
Well, for the most part now
Redundance in remembrance
That hers are the softest hands to hold
Hers is the sweetest coos to hear
True she said- I was in my head
Where her face never seems to change
She probably has grown old

I will never know.

12. Arrival

Hands waive themselves
Into nothingness
Seeking old warmth
Against your press
Seconds turn into/become days
Weeks, years, and centuries
(And) I count the time/I sit counting time
By (ripening) cycles of mulberries
With colors of blood and bruises
Fallen to the ground
Feet have blistered themselves
Pacing endlessly for years
To carve out a path
For you to not miss
The turn to our home
Path laden with leaves
To rustle around
And let me know/tell me
Of/about your arrival
Like a sweet spring
Or scorching summer
Misty rain or dry/cozy winter

Settling upon/on my skin/flesh
As pollen, sunlight
raindrop or snowfall.
Eyes tired/have tired themselves
Searching for your shadows/
Against the rusty horizon
In your wait, I carry/(still) feel
The lightness of your hand
Resting on my chest
Like a feather/cloud in the wind
Going up, going down
Synced with labored breaths
(And) Burdened with dreams
That hasn't come true, yet.
Arms have thrown themselves
Into oblivion
The incentives I left
(Probably) Weren't/ aren't enough
My love, warmth,
And promises to be better
Waiting on porch
Hoping for return
Drenching/standing in the rain showers
Just the same
Lips have quivered themselves
(Endlessly)Excusing your delay/absence
I hope you come

But I know you too well
To know that you never will
That you never learned to learn
The ways of my care
The language of my love
Redemption and repentance
Have lucked out again
I feel/think that you never
Wanted/Learnt to stay.
So, when you arrive my way
To love, laugh, and stay
With arms that want to hold me
And the chest to bury my face and sob
Be carved out of rock
For I think it will be another lifetime
That I'll be able to stop.

13. Paradox

She is the fire,
That burns and bakes,
Melts and hardens.
She is the water too,
Weakening and strengthening.
She is the blood so crimson,
Thick as honey,
Flooding the sewers.
The plea,
Of mercy and death.
That ink blot,
Ugly yet meaningful.
The sourness of cream,
Distasteful and reality.
Recurring nightmare,
Scary but unreal.
The wounded tigress,
Vulnerable and ruthless.
The star,
Twinkling, diminishing and twinkling again.
The rust,
Killer, and waste.

The skipped beat,
Of Joyful and traumatized.
She is a multiverse
In the universe of people and places.
A paradox
Invisible and ever existing.
She is, but the darkest sheen.

14. You Were

You were waiting for me to come
Whisper in your ear my poem
Gently tucking in your hair,
Dandelions under the stars.
Moonlight falls on your face
Eyes shine brighter always
You listen to my words-
Dancing
With the sound of the Ganges
Passing through the pebbled pathways.

15. Here I

Here I stand.
With hope in one eye,
And tear in another.
An eye for an eye.
Whichever shall win,
Will be followed by the other.
Losing out on its own existence.
Burn the face carried for years.
Mask your true identity
For this world
Is no place for runner-ups.

16. The Missed Call

You're the incoming call
Flashing on my phone
I choose not to answer
And look the other way
With pangs of guilt and hurt
Each more than other
Gnawing my heart
I choose to bear
I choose to suffer
And when the ringing stops
I go back to my business of
Being busy doing nothing
You're the hot coffee
I made with such passion
And extra cubes
Of sugar and love
Which now feel the poison
Moments pass by
And it is now cold
I hold it and think
If I should drink
I decide otherwise

Flushing it down the sink
You're entangled hair
I washed yesterday
But didn't comb
Now it's late
And it's a hurtful process
To detangle
So I wait for the next day
To wash it again
And let the mess rest
On my head
You're the gift
I wanted more than anything
But did not need anyway
And once I had it
I lost the want
And now it lies
As a showpiece on my table
I barely notice it
As good as nothing
I kept it anyway
Hoarding
Like rest of your memories
You're the book
I started years ago
Never to complete
It sits on the (book) shelf

Dust settling/settles
Layer by layer
Never too away to not be noticed
I make false promises
To return/of returning to it someday
To pick up from where I left
To finish what was started
Knowing I would never
You're the lies and excuses
That sit on my tongue
Waiting to be slipped
To be trusted
Weaved out in conversations
That I/we stopped having
It doesn't matter
If I tell you the truth
Because you stopped
Listening
A long time ago
You're the red dress
That hangs for the last time
In my closet
Like a best-kept secret
Of our first night together
I think of giving it away
Keeping it only occupies
Space it doesn't deserve

They say love leaves
A lot after lovers go
It is only fair
Now that (my) beloved has left
Love should follow.

17. Milky Way

Bury me under the tinkering
Lights of Milky way
Choked under their weight
My living body lay.
Alive, kicking, and breathing
My heavy heart docile
Letting fingers dance
Counting scars and walking miles.
Tying the fairy lights of
A thousand thoughts and stars
Guiding me back home
Lest I float afar

18. Shore

Your absence is not
Absence of you
I carry you in my heart
And you carry too
Like souvenirs we collected
Shells on the seashore
I walk through the sands every day
Collecting you some more
My desire for you spans the ocean
My love spans the sky
Deeper than the trenches
And higher than high
I walk around and write your name
In the sands eternal
Even if the tides
Sweep us nocturnal
Picking the colours of
Dusk and dawn
Singing the sounds of waves
And bells along
I have built a rainbow
Brick by brick

Hue by hue
Collecting the pastels
Just for you
I'm waiting on the other side
For your gentle stride
Leaving the footmarks
Left and right
And I do know that
While you come
With feet like stones and
Heart like plum
But I ain't losing
Hope no more
Knowing you'd come
Crashing ashore

19. June Baby

It has been a long day
It will be a long night.
You are a June baby
Sleep tight.
Unmask all your faces
Come out of all cases
Coffins are for carcasses
And you all right
You're a June baby
Sleep tight.
Gaze at the stars
Pine from afar
Light your cigar
Beholding sight
You're a June baby
Sleep tight.

20. Bad O Bad

Hanging from the cliff.
May I rise, I see your face,
May I fall, death is sure.
But I am still,
I breathe and pant,
And murmur prayers
Under my breath.
You smirking evil,
Bad O Bad
My eyes drift far away,
I picture you on the horizon,
And in the vertical over the cliff.
Or is it you playing with my head?
You smirking evil,
Bad O Bad
I may just lose the grip,
Be fast and hold my hand.
Hold my hand and I will rise.
May I rise I see your face.
May I fall, death is sure.
But I am still,
I breathe and pant,

And murmur prayers
Under my breath.
You smirking evil,
Bad O Bad
Death may come and so may love.
Love may come and so may death.

21. When The Red Flowers Bloom

When the red flowers bloom
I shall then grieve.
Moving my body
To the sound of my heartbeat.
I shall mourn the ones I've lost
To hatred, fear, and jealousy.
And count what it had cost
To create a real fallacy.
Letting it all flow
The sweat, saliva, and sadness.
Scratching the surface of the sane heart
Giving in to the madness.
When the red flowers bloom
When the red flowers bloom.

22. Color of Love

The color of love isn't red, pink, or mauve
Love doesn't smell of roses or jasmine or lilies
It is not best said in lexicons and languages
It doesn't always come packed in pretty boxes
On anniversaries and birthdays
It isn't always a ring in a box
Or a man on his knees.
Love comes every day.
Sometimes as pastel color of his shirts
Or his musky scents
And garlic breaths
In unspoken words and sober silence
In unmade but fulfilled promises
Not too loud
But gentle to the eyes and heart.

23. When Two People Meet

It's a sight when two people,
Lesser-known and un-bothered
Just like the poles,
Collide momentarily in this/the
(Ever)scheming and uncaring universe,
Fit into each other's hand(s)
lick each other's wounds.
Wash each other for their sins.
Lifting the crippling weights off their chests.
Bit by bit, one pebble at a time.
Until the pain becomes bearable
(The temperament is pacified)
And the dead emotions resurface.
Scraping the moss off the long unused and carefully packed feels(feelings)
As the secrets slip off their tongues into the other's mouth,
Tasting bittersweet.
They let the puzzling pieces fall into places,
At slow paces as their lips play tug and war.
Hurrying would make the moment cease to exist.

But keeping it slow is like keeping still when
a thousand Tsunamis hit you
All at once.
Dislodging the sand beneath the feet
While they stand there trying to claw deeper.
Fragile, and tender and strong,
All at once.
With all the volcanoes erupting
And the world coming to an end,
They're the flowing lava,
The melted rock meeting the pacific.
Calm as the eye of the hurricane,
They are the death stare into the eyes of death.
The two people,
Defining/creating a universe for each other.

24. Canadian Summer

Why break the ice?
It is hard and sharp and cold.
Beneath the thickness lies
A thousand stories are untold.
Don't/why bother knowing what goes
Inside that beautiful mind.
That who/what was carried forward and
who/what was/were left behind?
Let the ice remain intact
The bottoms of the sea are warmer.
Continue with the forbidden contact
And wait for the Canadian summer.

25. Deviants

Let us hold our breaths till we pant,
Burn till we are ashes.
Stop existing till we vanish.
We are the deviants, the liabilities.
But let us do this world a favor,
The first and last by us.
Let us skin each other,
Or melt the flesh off our bones.
Choose the painful for we should be punished to deviate.
Let us gift a monochromatic world to the synced robots.

Bestseller Books By 'kailashi' Punit D.

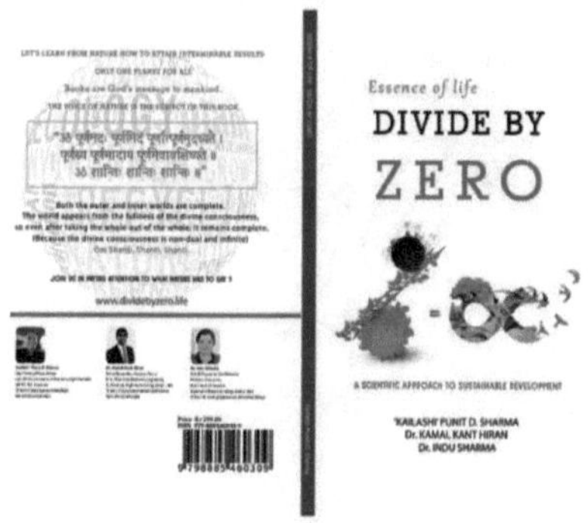

Essence of Life - Divide By Zero 'A Scientific Approach to Sustainable Development'

AUTHOR- 'KAILASHI' PUNIT D., DR. KAMAL KANT HIRAN & DR. INDU SHARMA

ISBN-9798885460309

PUBLISHER- NOTION PRESS CHENNAI, INDIA

BESTSELLER BOOKS BY 'KAILASHI' PUNIT D.

‘KAVYANJALI’- JEEVAN EK MOUN ABHIVAYAKTI

AUTHOR- ‘KAILASHI’ PUNIT D. & LAVINA SHARMA

ISBN-9781684879434

PUBLISHER- NOTION PRESS CHENNAI, INDIA

9 798885 550833

Printed by Libri Plureos GmbH in Hamburg, Germany